A

TOOLBOX

for Building a Better Life
after Incarceration

Foryst Ralph Hutchinson

BOOK PUBLISHERS NETWORK

Book Publishers Network
P.O. Box 2256
Bothell • WA • 98041
Ph • 425-483-3040
www.bookpublishersnetwork.com

10 9 8 7 6 5 4 3 2 1

Printed in the United States of America

LCCN 2008943471
ISBN10 1-935359-07-X
ISBN13 978-1-935359-07-4

Editor: Julie Scandora
Typographer: Stephanie Martindale

To my son, Jason, and the Penman family

CONTENTS

ACKNOWLEDGEMENTS

I thank my Aunt Mary Ann Hutchinson and my Uncle Kenneth Hutchinson for helping me put all of my writings into a presentable format. I am especially grateful for their utmost support and confidence in me and my book. I thank you from the bottom of my heart.

Next, I thank Dr. Jerry Meints for his professional evaluation and honesty about my book. His advice guided me in the correct direction and gave me the motivation to see this project through. I also thank him for allowing me to use some of his "Men's Tools" words.

I give thanks to Harry Truman and Zig Ziglar, who I have quoted in this book, for their great motivational inspiration.

And most of all, I thank my mother, Jean Stits, for her honest opinions throughout my ordeal and my book. I thank her dearly every day. We are each other's support system.

FORYST RALPH HUTCHINSON

INTRODUCTION

On September 23, 2006, at the age of fifty-four, my life changed forever. Due to wrong choices and a sick and dysfunctional relationship, I found myself in the system charged with a felony and looking at nine to fifteen years and two strikes. I plea bargained to two years with half time and one strike. I went to the California State Prison in Calipatria for thirteen long months.

A prison experience makes a man hard in spirit and deprives him of an identity. I am convinced that these attitudes can be turned around, given a change of heart. Most important for me, I found sobriety in AA along with having Jesus Christ in my life. These two things have changed my life.

While in prison, I came to realize there are some real needs among the inmates. Because I am an educated man, my fellow inmates reached out to me for help in passing the GED. Sixteen men out of nineteen with just an eighth- or ninth-grade education were able to succeed at getting their GEDs. I helped them and found much satisfaction and joy in this.

Now that I am rebuilding my life, I have faced many challenges and continue to face them each day. Because of the good feelings that came to me while I was helping others behind bars, I now want to help the individual that has a desire to rebuild his life with the necessary advice and directions that have helped me since I have been on parole. I feel AA, along with the Lord, is directing my path, and *A Toolbox for Building a Better Life after Incarceration* is the product of that inspiration.

I am motivated from:

 A sincere desire to help people.

FORYST RALPH HUTCHINSON

An inspiration from God and a sober mindset.

A genuine love for people and a desire to see their lives change for the better and for the good of society.

A passion to see others have an easier time, knowing where to go and what to do, so their motivation to change is not stolen by the sheer amount of investigative work.

The potential for personal financial freedom, so I can repay those who have unselfishly assisted me.

The potential positive feedback others may give me from using the tools and materials presented in my book.

The belief that the information presented in my Toolbox will be of great benefit to those who sincerely want to work toward and have a desire for a better life.

The fact that this packaged information is not available to former inmates and this comprehensive information fills a real need.

If you desire a new life and a second chance and are willing to work hard to better yourself, then *A Toolbox for Building a Better Life after Incarceration* is for you. We can turn this negative experience into a positive one. Staying clean and sober is the foundation to building a new life.

I hope by reading my material, you can get the feeling of a different approach to life than what you had before. The potential for change is in all of us. We just ignore it. I ask that you grasp this information and take it to heart because it has helped me, and I know it will help you.

God bless you, women and men.

HAMMER IN THIS MUST-DO LIST AS SOON AS POSSIBLE

- Contact CPS (Child Protection Services) to see what you need to do for visitation rights. If there isn't a "no contact" order or a "restraining" order on you, then contact your spouse or ex-spouse to set up days that you can see your child or children.

- Attend AA, and/or NA very quickly! This will help you keep a positive attitude. Plus it is a great place to meet people who may know of a job opening or a company looking for workers.

- If one of your conditions is to check into a half-way house, please do not drag your feet on this. CHECK IN. Space is hard to come by, and if you are a day or two late, you could lose your spot!

- By all means, carry a pen or pencil and paper. A note pad is good. That way you can write your appointment dates down and not forget them. My Grandfather always said "Do not make a scratchpad of your brain."

- Certain places require you to make an appointment, so do that before you inquire about a job. But others don't, and you can just go there.

Take one item at a time. Don't get excited and try to do everything at once.

FORYST RALPH HUTCHINSON

1

WRENCH THESE NECESSARY ITEMS IN PLACE

F Bus schedule
Make sure you have bus schedules for the bus routes that run close to you and for those that go where you are most likely to look for jobs.

F ID
Make sure you have a current ID or contact DMV (Department of Motor Vehicles) to get a driver's license or ID.

F Social Security Card

F Food
You need it; make sure it's healthy.

F Shelter
If you're rooming with others, make sure they are a positive influence on you.

F Clothing
Make sure you have some outfits that are appropriate for looking for a job and for working in the type of job you want.

F Job
Get it!

BEHAVIORS THAT WILL LOCK THE DOOR TO SUCCESS

Beware of riding in other people's vehicles! They could contain items that could cause you to violate your condition of parole very easily. Some of these are:

BB guns

Pellet guns

Squirt guns

Rubber-band guns

Pocket knives

Hunting knives

DEFINITELY all real guns. Even one empty shell casing will put you back behind bars

Live round

Baseball bat...alone. If the mitt is with the bat, you might have a chance....maybe.

Axe or machete

There are so many more. And the same is true about going into a person's home. Beware even of kids' toys! Who would ever think that we can go back to prison for a lousy squirt gun?

Most of all, if you are a passenger in a car and your buddy has an empty beer can or an empty pint bottle, and you are stopped by a police officer, you WILL be arrested.

Being around drugs is very dangerous. Avoid them and avoid being where they even might be.

The main thing is: BE AWARE OF YOUR SURROUND-INGS. Look at your life as if you have a Sky-Cam on you twenty-four hours a day. Never turn this off. Keep it trickling on at night. When you wake up, kick your Sky-Cam on and just be careful, be aware, and most of all, stay up-beat and avoid negative people!

Check out your attitude. When I was in prison, I learned that when a situation arose with me and another individual, I HAD to take care of that RIGHT THEN. If I didn't, I was a punk, and then I had real problems to face. I took care or confronted matters immediately.

But when I was paroled, I noticed the respect that I had earned vanished. People were rude, arrogant, and unpleasant. I had to overlook a lot of situations because the public doesn't have any idea what I went through.

You'll find out the same thing. You'll want to tell what you have been through. But they won't really listen, and they just wouldn't understand, and they will deny that you went through anything at all.

I have confronted people and pled my case. They think I was in a cell— alone—and that's that. So I write this to tell you to turn the other cheek, forget trying to explain what you went through and expecting understanding and move on. Go forward, because your life WILL get better. Stay positive and focused and check into all your conditional places, and you will be OK.

With AA, NA, and God, you will survive and be a better person. You WILL succeed.

BEHAVIORS THAT WILL LOCK THE DOOR TO SUCCESS

- Listening to the negative opinions and put-downs of others, such as "You can't do that!"

- Giving into to fear.

- Procrastinating important duties and meetings.

- Not going to AA and NA meetings.

- Doing drugs and alcohol.

- Not being completely honest with yourself and others.

- Giving up after being rejected from a job search.

- Not sticking to a task that is difficult or unpleasant (such as waiting in line).

- Going out of your county or designated area.

- Not following safe driving practices.

- Going to a drug area or loitering in front of a liquor store.

- Associating with other felons that drag you down.

- Not paying parking tickets or any ticket.

- Dressing inappropriately or having bad hygiene.

- Not covering your tattoos.

- Making bad choices and decisions.

- Refusing treatment or help at a half-way house.

- Forgetting that this situation is not forever.

BEHAVIORS THAT ARE THE KEY TO SUCCESS

Learn not to curse or use profanity ("bad" words). I came from a place where even the guards cursed 24/7. It's very hard to stop, but if I wanted a job, I had to have my interview to go well, and I could not use bad words or even "hey, man." Practice talking in front of a mirror to prepare for interviews.

Positive thinking is a strong tool.

If you are focused and on a mission, you are strong and invincible. Tell yourself, "I CAN DO IT. I WILL FIND A JOB. I WILL GET AN APARTMENT," or whatever you need.

When you go to bed, just before you close your eyes, tell yourself, "I will get a job, I will find a place to live, etc."

Make yourself a daily goal the night before. Use my check-off sheet. Just by doing one or two things each day, you will start to feel good about yourself and that you *can* accomplish the tasks at hand.

These are behaviors you can do that will lead you to success:

- Make new friends among positive, upbeat, hard working people.

- Keep learning, even if you learn one new thing or new word a week that is not connected to your work or life.

- Exercise your body. You will feel energized.

- Find a joyful pastime—a few minutes of music, a walk, time alone for twenty minutes, or playing Frisbee with your dog.

- Be a child with your children. Laugh and play with them.

- When you have a petty grievance with your job, think of a good thing about the work and balance it out.

- Do some community service. You will feel so good helping someone, and it will raise your self-esteem.

- When you are being treated rudely, say in a store, smile back. You'll be surprised with how it can change the person's mood.

- Treat every person you meet with respect. You never know how that person may play a good role in your new life.

- Keep healthy. When you are well, you "glow."

- Stand tall. Posture gives you dignity.

- Go to work a little early. Bosses notice and see that you are dedicated.

- Don't complain about or gossip about other workers. When you stay above negative talk, you gain everyone's trust.

- Give your neighbors their privacy, but be there to help when they need it. You may need the favor returned.

- If your family or friends are negative toward you, ignore it. Know that you are not that person. Only you know yourself, and *you are a good person.*

STAY SQUARE, STRAIGHT, AND TRUE

Talk without cursing or using "Hey, man," especially when job searching. This is hard to do, and speaking first hand, it takes practice to talk without slang. Try speaking to a mirror.

Certain children's toys will get you a violation and send you back to prison.

Find, or ask for, the need of a sponsor at NA or AA. This person will be your guide and mentor. Look for a sponsor who is five years or more in recovery and working a program. This is A SURE MUST for success.

Stay focused and honest! If you are having a hard time, let your AA or NA group know this. They will help with solid advice for your specific issues.

You CAN and you WILL make a difference. Keep repeating this to yourself in the morning and at night before you go to sleep. This will make it so.

As stated earlier, and I can't help but to say this again and again, ASK THE LORD FOR HELP AND GUIDANCE.

HAVE A PLAN

You need a plan to build a house. To build a life, it is even more important to have a plan or goal.

- Zig Ziglar

WHO IS Zig Ziglar? A man who knows hard times. Living in the state of Alabama in 1932, his father died of a stroke and his younger sister died two days later, leaving his mother to raise the remaining eleven children alone. He is now a motivational speaker.

Each Night Pre-plan:

L Write down all the job contacts you have made with:
- name
- address
- phone number
- location
- date for your follow-up call, two to three days after your first contact

L Check your appointment calendar.

L Decide where you're going to look for work.

L Know what form of transportation you'll be taking and, if public transit, the schedule.

L Select the clothes you'll wear tomorrow.

L Enter your reflections of the day in your journal.

L Reread your dream job each evening before sleeping.

L Get to bed early.

Review your appointments from the day. If any of these need taking care of, add them to your plan for tomorrow.

Ask yourself:

A Did I check in with parole?

A Did I check in with a half-way house?

A Did I make an appointment with the places with "conditions" of parole or probation?

A Did I contact CPS (Child Protection Services) to set up visitation or meetings or to get my child or children back?

A Do I have any medical or dental issues that need to be taken care of?

A Did I make a big effort to go to AA, NA, and church? These are positive places to get "real" helpful advice and acceptance.

DAILY DISCIPLINES

In reading the lives of great men, I found that the first victory they won was over **themselves***... self-discipline with all of them came first.*

- Harry S. Truman
33rd President

Do these everyday.

1. Awake early, 6:00 AM or earlier, whether you **feel** like it or not!

   I get up at 5:00 AM and go to my 5:30 AM AA meeting every other day. This gives my day a big boost and starts my day off with a positive spirit. If I have a very negative event in my life, I might go daily. **When I do not want to go is when I need the meeting the most!**

2. Personal Grooming: Shave (if a man), shower/bathe, brush teeth, comb or style your hair then dress in clean clothes appropriate for the day's planned activities. The main goal with your appearance is to make a positive first impression!
   Appropriate clothes for:
   Desk or Sales Job
   Men: Slacks, button-up shirt with tie, dress shoes.
   Women: Well-pressed, clean and neat dress or skirt and blouse, dress shoes.
   Construction or More Physical Job
   Men: Levis with no holes or stains, clean t-shirt with no holes or stains, and boots.

Women: Clean slacks with no holes or stains, clean and stain-free blouse or t-shirt, tennis shoes or work boots.

It is a good idea to bring both styles of clothing with you so you can change and go to as many job interviews as possible in a day.

3. Eat a nutritious breakfast. This will fuel your body and help you think clearly.

4. Look at your calendar. Enter in all the appointments and classes you are required to attend, such as DMV, parole, GED classes, etc.

5. Make follow-up calls two to three days later for all of the places that you visited looking for a job. And use good language. For example:

"Hello my name is _____. I applied several days ago for the position of _____. I am still very interested in the job and available for an interview."

Politely ask the receptionist to document the fact that you called by taking down your name and phone number. If you do arrange an interview, check your calendar to make sure you have no conflicts and write down the time and place on the day you have set.

6. Keep a positive outlook and look pleased when filling out applications and when talking to the secretary or receptionist. She can be the one that puts in a good word for you—or tells the boss not to bother. Look each person in the eye and be courteous at all times. Wherever you go, ask if anyone is hiring. The job may not be your dream job, but each one will give you

experience and may open doors in positive directions, eventually taking you to the one you want.

7. Reread your dream job. Do something each day to further this dream. Make a phone call or attend a class. Do something each day.

8. When you go on job interviews and must take public transportation, make a note of what buses or public vehicle you ride to get to that specific location as well as cross streets.

9. STAY POSITIVE. This is challenging work. Like lifting weights, it might seem a push in the beginning, but the more you do it, the easier it gets. It is not that the weight gets lighter, but *your ability improves.*

REWARDS WILL HAPPEN WITH PLANNED DISCIPLINE.

DREAM JOB

Enter your dream job in the Success Journal, the pages that follow this. Make your dream happen by looking into trade schools, night schools, or colleges. (Trade schools you might consider are: truck driving, carpentry, medical fields, machinist, auto, grocery, chef, etc.) Or be your own boss if that is your dream. Chart your course by writing the steps of what it will take to make your dream happen. Once you have a plan, work your plan and check off the items as you accomplish each step.

Date: _____

My dream job is

_____

What will I have to do to meet this goal?

1. _____

2. _____

3. _____

4. _____

5. _____

6. _____

7. _____

Add as many steps as you need to reach your goal. You may have to add more as you go along and discover what more you must do.

SUCCESS JOURNAL

The following 60 pages are a daily "check-off and fill-in-the-blanks" review of each day. Before the pages run out, make copies of one of the blank pages and continue to write your review the happenings of each day.

DATE _____

THE KEY TO SUCCESS IS AWARENESS

ANSWER THESE QUESTIONS EVERY DAY

Yes No Did I listen to the negative opinions and put downs of others?

Yes No Did I show courage and not give in to my fears?

Yes No Did I avoid procrastinating important duties and meetings?

Yes No Did I attend my AA and/or NA meetings

Yes No For today did I avoid doing drugs and alcohol?

Yes No Was I completely honest with myself and others?

Yes No Did I give up after being rejected from a job search?

Yes No Did I go out of my county or designated area?

Yes No Did I follow safe driving practices?

Yes No Did I go into a drug area or loiter in front of a liquor store?

Yes No Did I associate with other felons who could drag me down?

Yes No Did I dress appropriately and have good hygiene today?

A good decision that I made today

_____

_____

_____

_____

_____

_____

Today I am grateful for

_____

_____

_____

_____

_____

_____

SUCCESS JOURNAL

DATE _____

THE KEY TO SUCCESS IS AWARENESS

ANSWER THESE QUESTIONS EVERY DAY

Yes No Did I listen to the negative opinions and put downs of others?

Yes No Did I show courage and not give in to my fears?

Yes No Did I avoid procrastinating important duties and meetings?

Yes No Did I attend my AA and/or NA meetings

Yes No For today did I avoid doing drugs and alcohol?

Yes No Was I completely honest with myself and others?

Yes No Did I give up after being rejected from a job search?

Yes No Did I go out of my county or designated area?

Yes No Did I follow safe driving practices?

Yes No Did I go into a drug area or loiter in front of a liquor store?

Yes No Did I associate with other felons who could drag me down?

Yes No Did I dress appropriately and have good hygiene today?

A good decision that I made today

_____

_____

_____

_____

_____

_____

Today I am grateful for

_____

_____

_____

_____

_____

_____

_____

SUCCESS JOURNAL

DATE _____

THE KEY TO SUCCESS IS AWARENESS

ANSWER THESE QUESTIONS EVERY DAY

Yes No Did I listen to the negative opinions and put downs of others?

Yes No Did I show courage and not give in to my fears?

Yes No Did I avoid procrastinating important duties and meetings?

Yes No Did I attend my AA and/or NA meetings

Yes No For today did I avoid doing drugs and alcohol?

Yes No Was I completely honest with myself and others?

Yes No Did I give up after being rejected from a job search?

Yes No Did I go out of my county or designated area?

Yes No Did I follow safe driving practices?

Yes No Did I go into a drug area or loiter in front of a liquor store?

Yes No Did I associate with other felons who could drag me down?

Yes No Did I dress appropriately and have good hygiene today?

A good decision that I made today

_____

_____

_____

_____

_____

_____

Today I am grateful for

_____

_____

_____

_____

_____

_____

SUCCESS JOURNAL

DATE _____

THE KEY TO SUCCESS IS AWARENESS

ANSWER THESE QUESTIONS EVERY DAY

Yes No Did I listen to the negative opinions and put downs of others?

Yes No Did I show courage and not give in to my fears?

Yes No Did I avoid procrastinating important duties and meetings?

Yes No Did I attend my AA and/or NA meetings

Yes No For today did I avoid doing drugs and alcohol?

Yes No Was I completely honest with myself and others?

Yes No Did I give up after being rejected from a job search?

Yes No Did I go out of my county or designated area?

Yes No Did I follow safe driving practices?

Yes No Did I go into a drug area or loiter in front of a liquor store?

Yes No Did I associate with other felons who could drag me down?

Yes No Did I dress appropriately and have good hygiene today?

A good decision that I made today

_____

_____

_____

_____

_____

_____

Today I am grateful for

_____

_____

_____

_____

_____

_____

SUCCESS JOURNAL

DATE _____

THE KEY TO SUCCESS IS AWARENESS

ANSWER THESE QUESTIONS EVERY DAY

Yes No Did I listen to the negative opinions and put downs of others?

Yes No Did I show courage and not give in to my fears?

Yes No Did I avoid procrastinating important duties and meetings?

Yes No Did I attend my AA and/or NA meetings

Yes No For today did I avoid doing drugs and alcohol?

Yes No Was I completely honest with myself and others?

Yes No Did I give up after being rejected from a job search?

Yes No Did I go out of my county or designated area?

Yes No Did I follow safe driving practices?

Yes No Did I go into a drug area or loiter in front of a liquor store?

Yes No Did I associate with other felons who could drag me down?

Yes No Did I dress appropriately and have good hygiene today?

A good decision that I made today

_____

_____

_____

_____

_____

_____

Today I am grateful for

_____

_____

_____

_____

_____

_____

SUCCESS JOURNAL

DATE _____

THE KEY TO SUCCESS IS AWARENESS

ANSWER THESE QUESTIONS EVERY DAY

Yes No Did I listen to the negative opinions and put downs of others?

Yes No Did I show courage and not give in to my fears?

Yes No Did I avoid procrastinating important duties and meetings?

Yes No Did I attend my AA and/or NA meetings

Yes No For today did I avoid doing drugs and alcohol?

Yes No Was I completely honest with myself and others?

Yes No Did I give up after being rejected from a job search?

Yes No Did I go out of my county or designated area?

Yes No Did I follow safe driving practices?

Yes No Did I go into a drug area or loiter in front of a liquor store?

Yes No Did I associate with other felons who could drag me down?

Yes No Did I dress appropriately and have good hygiene today?

A good decision that I made today

_____

_____

_____

_____

_____

_____

Today I am grateful for

_____

_____

_____

_____

_____

_____

SUCCESS JOURNAL

DATE _____

THE KEY TO SUCCESS IS AWARENESS

ANSWER THESE QUESTIONS EVERY DAY

Yes No Did I listen to the negative opinions and put downs of others?

Yes No Did I show courage and not give in to my fears?

Yes No Did I avoid procrastinating important duties and meetings?

Yes No Did I attend my AA and/or NA meetings

Yes No For today did I avoid doing drugs and alcohol?

Yes No Was I completely honest with myself and others?

Yes No Did I give up after being rejected from a job search?

Yes No Did I go out of my county or designated area?

Yes No Did I follow safe driving practices?

Yes No Did I go into a drug area or loiter in front of a liquor store?

Yes No Did I associate with other felons who could drag me down?

Yes No Did I dress appropriately and have good hygiene today?

A good decision that I made today

_____

_____

_____

_____

_____

_____

Today I am grateful for

_____

_____

_____

_____

_____

_____

SUCCESS JOURNAL

DATE _____

THE KEY TO SUCCESS IS AWARENESS

ANSWER THESE QUESTIONS EVERY DAY

Yes No Did I listen to the negative opinions and put downs of others?

Yes No Did I show courage and not give in to my fears?

Yes No Did I avoid procrastinating important duties and meetings?

Yes No Did I attend my AA and/or NA meetings

Yes No For today did I avoid doing drugs and alcohol?

Yes No Was I completely honest with myself and others?

Yes No Did I give up after being rejected from a job search?

Yes No Did I go out of my county or designated area?

Yes No Did I follow safe driving practices?

Yes No Did I go into a drug area or loiter in front of a liquor store?

Yes No Did I associate with other felons who could drag me down?

Yes No Did I dress appropriately and have good hygiene today?

A good decision that I made today

_____

_____

_____

_____

_____

_____

Today I am grateful for

_____

_____

_____

_____

_____

_____

SUCCESS JOURNAL

DATE _____

THE KEY TO SUCCESS IS AWARENESS

ANSWER THESE QUESTIONS EVERY DAY

Yes No Did I listen to the negative opinions and put downs of others?

Yes No Did I show courage and not give in to my fears?

Yes No Did I avoid procrastinating important duties and meetings?

Yes No Did I attend my AA and/or NA meetings

Yes No For today did I avoid doing drugs and alcohol?

Yes No Was I completely honest with myself and others?

Yes No Did I give up after being rejected from a job search?

Yes No Did I go out of my county or designated area?

Yes No Did I follow safe driving practices?

Yes No Did I go into a drug area or loiter in front of a liquor store?

Yes No Did I associate with other felons who could drag me down?

Yes No Did I dress appropriately and have good hygiene today?

A good decision that I made today

_____

_____

_____

_____

_____

_____

Today I am grateful for

_____

_____

_____

_____

_____

_____

SUCCESS JOURNAL

DATE _____

THE KEY TO SUCCESS IS AWARENESS

ANSWER THESE QUESTIONS EVERY DAY

Yes No Did I listen to the negative opinions and put downs of others?

Yes No Did I show courage and not give in to my fears?

Yes No Did I avoid procrastinating important duties and meetings?

Yes No Did I attend my AA and/or NA meetings

Yes No For today did I avoid doing drugs and alcohol?

Yes No Was I completely honest with myself and others?

Yes No Did I give up after being rejected from a job search?

Yes No Did I go out of my county or designated area?

Yes No Did I follow safe driving practices?

Yes No Did I go into a drug area or loiter in front of a liquor store?

Yes No Did I associate with other felons who could drag me down?

Yes No Did I dress appropriately and have good hygiene today?

A good decision that I made today

_____

_____

_____

_____

_____

_____

Today I am grateful for

_____

_____

_____

_____

_____

_____

_____

SUCCESS JOURNAL

DATE _____

THE KEY TO SUCCESS IS AWARENESS

ANSWER THESE QUESTIONS EVERY DAY

Yes No Did I listen to the negative opinions and put downs of others?

Yes No Did I show courage and not give in to my fears?

Yes No Did I avoid procrastinating important duties and meetings?

Yes No Did I attend my AA and/or NA meetings

Yes No For today did I avoid doing drugs and alcohol?

Yes No Was I completely honest with myself and others?

Yes No Did I give up after being rejected from a job search?

Yes No Did I go out of my county or designated area?

Yes No Did I follow safe driving practices?

Yes No Did I go into a drug area or loiter in front of a liquor store?

Yes No Did I associate with other felons who could drag me down?

Yes No Did I dress appropriately and have good hygiene today?

A good decision that I made today

_____

_____

_____

_____

_____

_____

Today I am grateful for

_____

_____

_____

_____

_____

_____

SUCCESS JOURNAL

DATE _____

THE KEY TO SUCCESS IS AWARENESS

ANSWER THESE QUESTIONS EVERY DAY

Yes No Did I listen to the negative opinions and put downs of others?

Yes No Did I show courage and not give in to my fears?

Yes No Did I avoid procrastinating important duties and meetings?

Yes No Did I attend my AA and/or NA meetings

Yes No For today did I avoid doing drugs and alcohol?

Yes No Was I completely honest with myself and others?

Yes No Did I give up after being rejected from a job search?

Yes No Did I go out of my county or designated area?

Yes No Did I follow safe driving practices?

Yes No Did I go into a drug area or loiter in front of a liquor store?

Yes No Did I associate with other felons who could drag me down?

Yes No Did I dress appropriately and have good hygiene today?

A good decision that I made today

_____

_____

_____

_____

_____

_____

Today I am grateful for

_____

_____

_____

_____

_____

_____

SUCCESS JOURNAL

DATE _____

THE KEY TO SUCCESS IS AWARENESS

ANSWER THESE QUESTIONS EVERY DAY

Yes No Did I listen to the negative opinions and put downs of others?

Yes No Did I show courage and not give in to my fears?

Yes No Did I avoid procrastinating important duties and meetings?

Yes No Did I attend my AA and/or NA meetings

Yes No For today did I avoid doing drugs and alcohol?

Yes No Was I completely honest with myself and others?

Yes No Did I give up after being rejected from a job search?

Yes No Did I go out of my county or designated area?

Yes No Did I follow safe driving practices?

Yes No Did I go into a drug area or loiter in front of a liquor store?

Yes No Did I associate with other felons who could drag me down?

Yes No Did I dress appropriately and have good hygiene today?

A good decision that I made today

_____

_____

_____

_____

_____

_____

Today I am grateful for

_____

_____

_____

_____

_____

_____

SUCCESS JOURNAL

DATE _____

THE KEY TO SUCCESS IS AWARENESS

ANSWER THESE QUESTIONS EVERY DAY

Yes No Did I listen to the negative opinions and put downs of others?

Yes No Did I show courage and not give in to my fears?

Yes No Did I avoid procrastinating important duties and meetings?

Yes No Did I attend my AA and/or NA meetings

Yes No For today did I avoid doing drugs and alcohol?

Yes No Was I completely honest with myself and others?

Yes No Did I give up after being rejected from a job search?

Yes No Did I go out of my county or designated area?

Yes No Did I follow safe driving practices?

Yes No Did I go into a drug area or loiter in front of a liquor store?

Yes No Did I associate with other felons who could drag me down?

Yes No Did I dress appropriately and have good hygiene today?

A good decision that I made today

_____

_____

_____

_____

_____

Today I am grateful for

_____

_____

_____

_____

_____

_____

SUCCESS JOURNAL

DATE _____

THE KEY TO SUCCESS IS AWARENESS

ANSWER THESE QUESTIONS EVERY DAY

Yes No Did I listen to the negative opinions and put downs of others?

Yes No Did I show courage and not give in to my fears?

Yes No Did I avoid procrastinating important duties and meetings?

Yes No Did I attend my AA and/or NA meetings

Yes No For today did I avoid doing drugs and alcohol?

Yes No Was I completely honest with myself and others?

Yes No Did I give up after being rejected from a job search?

Yes No Did I go out of my county or designated area?

Yes No Did I follow safe driving practices?

Yes No Did I go into a drug area or loiter in front of a liquor store?

Yes No Did I associate with other felons who could drag me down?

Yes No Did I dress appropriately and have good hygiene today?

A good decision that I made today

_____

_____

_____

_____

_____

_____

Today I am grateful for

_____

_____

_____

_____

_____

_____

SUCCESS JOURNAL

DATE _____

THE KEY TO SUCCESS IS AWARENESS

ANSWER THESE QUESTIONS EVERY DAY

Yes No Did I listen to the negative opinions and put downs of others?

Yes No Did I show courage and not give in to my fears?

Yes No Did I avoid procrastinating important duties and meetings?

Yes No Did I attend my AA and/or NA meetings

Yes No For today did I avoid doing drugs and alcohol?

Yes No Was I completely honest with myself and others?

Yes No Did I give up after being rejected from a job search?

Yes No Did I go out of my county or designated area?

Yes No Did I follow safe driving practices?

Yes No Did I go into a drug area or loiter in front of a liquor store?

Yes No Did I associate with other felons who could drag me down?

Yes No Did I dress appropriately and have good hygiene today?

A good decision that I made today

_____

_____

_____

_____

_____

_____

Today I am grateful for

_____

_____

_____

_____

_____

_____

_____

SUCCESS JOURNAL

DATE _____

THE KEY TO SUCCESS IS AWARENESS

ANSWER THESE QUESTIONS EVERY DAY

Yes No Did I listen to the negative opinions and put downs of others?

Yes No Did I show courage and not give in to my fears?

Yes No Did I avoid procrastinating important duties and meetings?

Yes No Did I attend my AA and/or NA meetings

Yes No For today did I avoid doing drugs and alcohol?

Yes No Was I completely honest with myself and others?

Yes No Did I give up after being rejected from a job search?

Yes No Did I go out of my county or designated area?

Yes No Did I follow safe driving practices?

Yes No Did I go into a drug area or loiter in front of a liquor store?

Yes No Did I associate with other felons who could drag me down?

Yes No Did I dress appropriately and have good hygiene today?

A good decision that I made today

_____

_____

_____

_____

_____

_____

Today I am grateful for

_____

_____

_____

_____

_____

_____

_____

SUCCESS JOURNAL

DATE _____

THE KEY TO SUCCESS IS AWARENESS

ANSWER THESE QUESTIONS EVERY DAY

Yes No Did I listen to the negative opinions and put downs of others?

Yes No Did I show courage and not give in to my fears?

Yes No Did I avoid procrastinating important duties and meetings?

Yes No Did I attend my AA and/or NA meetings

Yes No For today did I avoid doing drugs and alcohol?

Yes No Was I completely honest with myself and others?

Yes No Did I give up after being rejected from a job search?

Yes No Did I go out of my county or designated area?

Yes No Did I follow safe driving practices?

Yes No Did I go into a drug area or loiter in front of a liquor store?

Yes No Did I associate with other felons who could drag me down?

Yes No Did I dress appropriately and have good hygiene today?

A good decision that I made today

_____

_____

_____

_____

_____

_____

Today I am grateful for

_____

_____

_____

_____

_____

_____

SUCCESS JOURNAL

DATE _____

THE KEY TO SUCCESS IS AWARENESS

ANSWER THESE QUESTIONS EVERY DAY

Yes No Did I listen to the negative opinions and put downs of others?

Yes No Did I show courage and not give in to my fears?

Yes No Did I avoid procrastinating important duties and meetings?

Yes No Did I attend my AA and/or NA meetings

Yes No For today did I avoid doing drugs and alcohol?

Yes No Was I completely honest with myself and others?

Yes No Did I give up after being rejected from a job search?

Yes No Did I go out of my county or designated area?

Yes No Did I follow safe driving practices?

Yes No Did I go into a drug area or loiter in front of a liquor store?

Yes No Did I associate with other felons who could drag me down?

Yes No Did I dress appropriately and have good hygiene today?

A good decision that I made today

_____

_____

_____

_____

_____

_____

Today I am grateful for

_____

_____

_____

_____

_____

_____

_____

SUCCESS JOURNAL

DATE _____

THE KEY TO SUCCESS IS AWARENESS

ANSWER THESE QUESTIONS EVERY DAY

Yes No   Did I listen to the negative opinions and put downs of others?

Yes No   Did I show courage and not give in to my fears?

Yes No   Did I avoid procrastinating important duties and meetings?

Yes No   Did I attend my AA and/or NA meetings

Yes No   For today did I avoid doing drugs and alcohol?

Yes No   Was I completely honest with myself and others?

Yes No   Did I give up after being rejected from a job search?

Yes No   Did I go out of my county or designated area?

Yes No   Did I follow safe driving practices?

Yes No   Did I go into a drug area or loiter in front of a liquor store?

Yes No   Did I associate with other felons who could drag me down?

Yes No   Did I dress appropriately and have good hygiene today?

A good decision that I made today

_____

_____

_____

_____

_____

_____

Today I am grateful for

_____

_____

_____

_____

_____

_____

SUCCESS JOURNAL

DATE _____

THE KEY TO SUCCESS IS AWARENESS

ANSWER THESE QUESTIONS EVERY DAY

Yes No Did I listen to the negative opinions and put downs of others?

Yes No Did I show courage and not give in to my fears?

Yes No Did I avoid procrastinating important duties and meetings?

Yes No Did I attend my AA and/or NA meetings

Yes No For today did I avoid doing drugs and alcohol?

Yes No Was I completely honest with myself and others?

Yes No Did I give up after being rejected from a job search?

Yes No Did I go out of my county or designated area?

Yes No Did I follow safe driving practices?

Yes No Did I go into a drug area or loiter in front of a liquor store?

Yes No Did I associate with other felons who could drag me down?

Yes No Did I dress appropriately and have good hygiene today?

A good decision that I made today

_____

_____

_____

_____

_____

_____

Today I am grateful for

_____

_____

_____

_____

_____

_____

DATE _____

THE KEY TO SUCCESS IS AWARENESS

ANSWER THESE QUESTIONS EVERY DAY

Yes No Did I listen to the negative opinions and put downs of others?

Yes No Did I show courage and not give in to my fears?

Yes No Did I avoid procrastinating important duties and meetings?

Yes No Did I attend my AA and/or NA meetings

Yes No For today did I avoid doing drugs and alcohol?

Yes No Was I completely honest with myself and others?

Yes No Did I give up after being rejected from a job search?

Yes No Did I go out of my county or designated area?

Yes No Did I follow safe driving practices?

Yes No Did I go into a drug area or loiter in front of a liquor store?

Yes No Did I associate with other felons who could drag me down?

Yes No Did I dress appropriately and have good hygiene today?

A good decision that I made today

_____

_____

_____

_____

_____

_____

Today I am grateful for

_____

_____

_____

_____

_____

_____

_____

SUCCESS JOURNAL

DATE _____

THE KEY TO SUCCESS IS AWARENESS

ANSWER THESE QUESTIONS EVERY DAY

Yes No Did I listen to the negative opinions and put downs of others?

Yes No Did I show courage and not give in to my fears?

Yes No Did I avoid procrastinating important duties and meetings?

Yes No Did I attend my AA and/or NA meetings

Yes No For today did I avoid doing drugs and alcohol?

Yes No Was I completely honest with myself and others?

Yes No Did I give up after being rejected from a job search?

Yes No Did I go out of my county or designated area?

Yes No Did I follow safe driving practices?

Yes No Did I go into a drug area or loiter in front of a liquor store?

Yes No Did I associate with other felons who could drag me down?

Yes No Did I dress appropriately and have good hygiene today?

A good decision that I made today

_____

_____

_____

_____

_____

_____

Today I am grateful for

_____

_____

_____

_____

_____

_____

SUCCESS JOURNAL

DATE _____

THE KEY TO SUCCESS IS AWARENESS

ANSWER THESE QUESTIONS EVERY DAY

Yes No Did I listen to the negative opinions and put downs of others?

Yes No Did I show courage and not give in to my fears?

Yes No Did I avoid procrastinating important duties and meetings?

Yes No Did I attend my AA and/or NA meetings

Yes No For today did I avoid doing drugs and alcohol?

Yes No Was I completely honest with myself and others?

Yes No Did I give up after being rejected from a job search?

Yes No Did I go out of my county or designated area?

Yes No Did I follow safe driving practices?

Yes No Did I go into a drug area or loiter in front of a liquor store?

Yes No Did I associate with other felons who could drag me down?

Yes No Did I dress appropriately and have good hygiene today?

A good decision that I made today

_____

_____

_____

_____

_____

_____

Today I am grateful for

_____

_____

_____

_____

_____

_____

_____

SUCCESS JOURNAL

DATE _____

THE KEY TO SUCCESS IS AWARENESS

ANSWER THESE QUESTIONS EVERY DAY

Yes No Did I listen to the negative opinions and put downs of others?

Yes No Did I show courage and not give in to my fears?

Yes No Did I avoid procrastinating important duties and meetings?

Yes No Did I attend my AA and/or NA meetings

Yes No For today did I avoid doing drugs and alcohol?

Yes No Was I completely honest with myself and others?

Yes No Did I give up after being rejected from a job search?

Yes No Did I go out of my county or designated area?

Yes No Did I follow safe driving practices?

Yes No Did I go into a drug area or loiter in front of a liquor store?

Yes No Did I associate with other felons who could drag me down?

Yes No Did I dress appropriately and have good hygiene today?

A good decision that I made today

_____

_____

_____

_____

_____

_____

Today I am grateful for

_____

_____

_____

_____

_____

_____

SUCCESS JOURNAL

DATE _____

THE KEY TO SUCCESS IS AWARENESS

ANSWER THESE QUESTIONS EVERY DAY

Yes No Did I listen to the negative opinions and put downs of others?

Yes No Did I show courage and not give in to my fears?

Yes No Did I avoid procrastinating important duties and meetings?

Yes No Did I attend my AA and/or NA meetings

Yes No For today did I avoid doing drugs and alcohol?

Yes No Was I completely honest with myself and others?

Yes No Did I give up after being rejected from a job search?

Yes No Did I go out of my county or designated area?

Yes No Did I follow safe driving practices?

Yes No Did I go into a drug area or loiter in front of a liquor store?

Yes No Did I associate with other felons who could drag me down?

Yes No Did I dress appropriately and have good hygiene today?

A good decision that I made today

_____

_____

_____

_____

_____

_____

Today I am grateful for

_____

_____

_____

_____

_____

_____

_____

SUCCESS JOURNAL

DATE _____

THE KEY TO SUCCESS IS AWARENESS

ANSWER THESE QUESTIONS EVERY DAY

Yes No   Did I listen to the negative opinions and put downs of others?

Yes No   Did I show courage and not give in to my fears?

Yes No   Did I avoid procrastinating important duties and meetings?

Yes No   Did I attend my AA and/or NA meetings

Yes No   For today did I avoid doing drugs and alcohol?

Yes No   Was I completely honest with myself and others?

Yes No   Did I give up after being rejected from a job search?

Yes No   Did I go out of my county or designated area?

Yes No   Did I follow safe driving practices?

Yes No   Did I go into a drug area or loiter in front of a liquor store?

Yes No   Did I associate with other felons who could drag me down?

Yes No   Did I dress appropriately and have good hygiene today?

A good decision that I made today

_____

_____

_____

_____

_____

_____

Today I am grateful for

_____

_____

_____

_____

_____

_____

SUCCESS JOURNAL

DATE _____

THE KEY TO SUCCESS IS AWARENESS

ANSWER THESE QUESTIONS EVERY DAY

Yes No Did I listen to the negative opinions and put downs of others?

Yes No Did I show courage and not give in to my fears?

Yes No Did I avoid procrastinating important duties and meetings?

Yes No Did I attend my AA and/or NA meetings

Yes No For today did I avoid doing drugs and alcohol?

Yes No Was I completely honest with myself and others?

Yes No Did I give up after being rejected from a job search?

Yes No Did I go out of my county or designated area?

Yes No Did I follow safe driving practices?

Yes No Did I go into a drug area or loiter in front of a liquor store?

Yes No Did I associate with other felons who could drag me down?

Yes No Did I dress appropriately and have good hygiene today?

A good decision that I made today

_____

_____

_____

_____

_____

_____

Today I am grateful for

_____

_____

_____

_____

_____

_____

SUCCESS JOURNAL

DATE _____

THE KEY TO SUCCESS IS AWARENESS

ANSWER THESE QUESTIONS EVERY DAY

Yes No Did I listen to the negative opinions and put downs of others?

Yes No Did I show courage and not give in to my fears?

Yes No Did I avoid procrastinating important duties and meetings?

Yes No Did I attend my AA and/or NA meetings

Yes No For today did I avoid doing drugs and alcohol?

Yes No Was I completely honest with myself and others?

Yes No Did I give up after being rejected from a job search?

Yes No Did I go out of my county or designated area?

Yes No Did I follow safe driving practices?

Yes No Did I go into a drug area or loiter in front of a liquor store?

Yes No Did I associate with other felons who could drag me down?

Yes No Did I dress appropriately and have good hygiene today?

A good decision that I made today

_____

_____

_____

_____

_____

_____

Today I am grateful for

_____

_____

_____

_____

_____

_____

_____

SUCCESS JOURNAL

DATE _____

THE KEY TO SUCCESS IS AWARENESS

ANSWER THESE QUESTIONS EVERY DAY

Yes No Did I listen to the negative opinions and put downs of others?

Yes No Did I show courage and not give in to my fears?

Yes No Did I avoid procrastinating important duties and meetings?

Yes No Did I attend my AA and/or NA meetings

Yes No For today did I avoid doing drugs and alcohol?

Yes No Was I completely honest with myself and others?

Yes No Did I give up after being rejected from a job search?

Yes No Did I go out of my county or designated area?

Yes No Did I follow safe driving practices?

Yes No Did I go into a drug area or loiter in front of a liquor store?

Yes No Did I associate with other felons who could drag me down?

Yes No Did I dress appropriately and have good hygiene today?

A good decision that I made today

_____

_____

_____

_____

_____

_____

Today I am grateful for

_____

_____

_____

_____

_____

_____

_____

THOUGHTS FROM THE HEART

As you go about your new life and set and put into place your plans, you should see changes for the positive begin to happen. I always carry a small notepad and pencil for making lists and writing down positive thoughts that pop into my head. There will always be negative impressions and negative voices tempting me back into the old ways, but I ignore them and fill my days with positive goals.

I learn to plan ahead, write things down, think positively, look nice, talk nice, and be considerate. I have learned that I have a much better chance at a successful life when I behave in this way. As I give this lifestyle a chance, it can and will give me a chance back.

I have accepted AA and God in my life for guidance, and I am so thankful for all He has done for me. I turned my life over to God. I say my prayers, bless my family and pray for them. By doing just this, my life has changed, and yours will also with a little desire. Desiring a change in your life is the first step toward making that change! I need AA, and together with God, my life is fulfilling. I tried living life my selfish way and had lots of problems. Now with my new direction, life seems worthwhile, and I have a sense of happiness and peace. Opportunities and a brighter future are just around the corner.

A Toolbox for building a Better Life after Incarceration was created out of my desire and hope that I could make your path to a brighter future easier than mine has been. Realizing that nothing like this book is available, I have been prayerful and worked diligently to gather all the elements that I have found helpful and I think will help you. I am not an expert and make no claims of professional credentials. This work comes to you from one who has walked a similar path and wants to help another fellow neighbor build a better life.

God bless you in your venture, as you BUILD A BETTER LIFE for a better tomorrow.

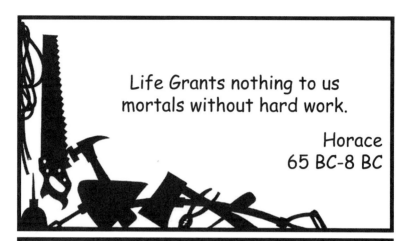

Life Grants nothing to us mortals without hard work.

Horace
65 BC-8 BC

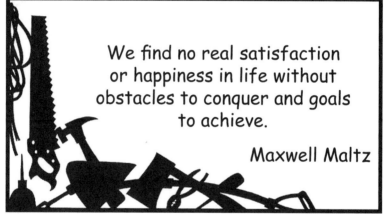

We find no real satisfaction or happiness in life without obstacles to conquer and goals to achieve.

Maxwell Maltz

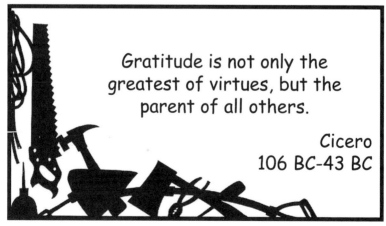

Gratitude is not only the greatest of virtues, but the parent of all others.

Cicero
106 BC-43 BC

A goal without a plan is
just a wish.

Antoine de Saint-Exupery
1900-1944

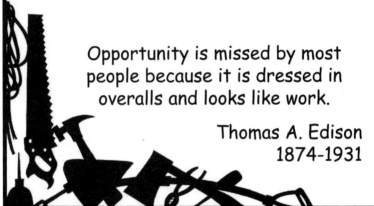

Opportunity is missed by most
people because it is dressed in
overalls and looks like work.

Thomas A. Edison
1874-1931

I have always thought the
actions of men the best
interpreters of their thoughts.

John Locke
1632-1704

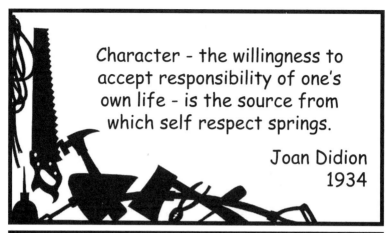

Character - the willingness to accept responsibility of one's own life - is the source from which self respect springs.

Joan Didion
1934

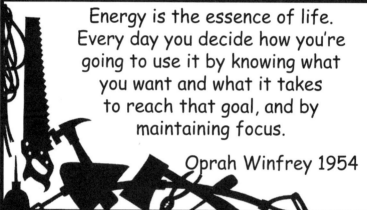

Energy is the essence of life. Every day you decide how you're going to use it by knowing what you want and what it takes to reach that goal, and by maintaining focus.

Oprah Winfrey 1954

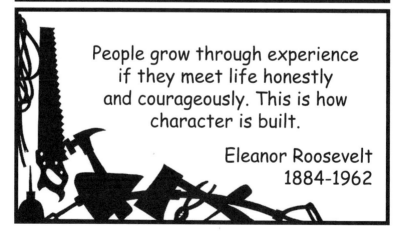

People grow through experience if they meet life honestly and courageously. This is how character is built.

Eleanor Roosevelt
1884-1962

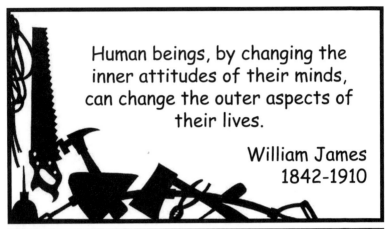

Human beings, by changing the inner attitudes of their minds, can change the outer aspects of their lives.

William James
1842-1910